BIRDS

Gareth Thomas

Illustrated by
Mike Atkinson

Kingfisher Books

Contents

Introduction	3
What to Look For	4
Attracting Birds into the Garden	8
Migration	10

IDENTIFICATION SECTION

Buildings and Gardens	12
Woodlands	20
Open Spaces	24
Moors and Heaths	30
Freshwaters	34
Coastal Areas	38
Nature Reserves	42
Bird Conservation	46
Where to Go From Here	47
Index	48

Kingfisher Books, Grisewood & Dempsey Ltd,
Elsley House, 24–30 Great Titchfield Street,
London W1P 7AD

This edition published in 1990 by Kingfisher Books.
First published in 1982 by Grisewood & Dempsey Ltd
as *St Michael Spotters: Birds*.
Revised edition published in 1985 in paperback by
Pan Books Ltd in the *Piccolo Spotters* series, and
in hardback by Kingfisher Books in the *Fun to Spot* series.
© Grisewood & Dempsey Ltd, 1982

All rights reserved

BRITISH LIBRARY CATALOGUING IN PUBLICATION DATA
Thomas, Gareth
 Birds.
 1. Great Britain. Birds. Field guides
 I. Title II. Atkinson, Michael III. Series
 598.2941
ISBN 0 86272 593 3

Phototypeset by Waveney Typesetters, Norwich
Printed in Portugal

Introduction

You may already be able to identify some of the birds you see. Flick through this book to see how many you know. If you are just starting to watch birds, this book will try to show you where to look for them, and the sort of things to spot and record.

The birds have been grouped according to where you are most likely to see them. However, remember that birds move around, and many may be seen in other places. One section describes some of the rarer birds which are mostly found in nature reserves.

For each bird described there are spaces for you to record the date and place where you first saw it, and what it was doing. For example, you may see a kestrel hovering, or a flock of wood pigeons flying to roost in the evening. If you are not sure of the name of a bird you see, do a quick field sketch (see page 5). Include any features of colour, shape or behaviour which you think will help you to identify it later on from this book. The average length from the beak to the end of the tail is given for each kind of bird.

It is a good idea to start bird-watching near your home. There is much you can do to attract birds into your garden (see pages 8 and 9). If you visit woods and other areas in the country, keep to the public areas and footpaths. Shut gates after you, and do ask permission before visiting private land.

A notebook and pencil are essential for bird-watchers. At some stage you may need a pair of binoculars. There are some very good, inexpensive binoculars on the market which will last a long time if well cared for. When choosing them it is best to get the advice of someone who knows about binoculars.

All birds, their nests and eggs are protected by law. When bird-watching remember not to disturb the birds and never damage their nests or eggs.

What to Look For

The information on the next few pages will give you some clues as to what to look for when bird spotting.

Note the size of the bird and compare it to birds you already know. Is it long and thin like a pied wagtail or rounded like a bullfinch? What are the main colours? Are there any particular marks such as eye stripes, wing bars, white rumps or outer tail feathers? Does it have a short beak and legs like a chaffinch or a long beak and legs like a curlew? Is the tail long like a magpie's or short and upright like a wren's?

Look at how it flies. Are the wings long and pointed or short and broad? Does the neck stick out as with the mallard? Or do the feet trail the body as with a flying heron? Record what you see as a quick field sketch. This will help you to identify the bird later.

GLOSSARY
Aggression Threatening behaviour; sometimes attack.
Carrion Dead and decaying animals.
Colony Place where many birds nest together.
Cover Concealment for a bird or its nest.
Displaying Moving in special ways that signal to other birds and enemies.
Falcon A small bird of prey.
Feral Captive birds that have returned to the wild.
Game bird A bird shot for food or sport, e.g. a pheasant.
Habitat Area where a bird lives, e.g. an oak wood.
Plumage All of a bird's feathers.
Predator Creature that kills others for food.
Roost The place where birds sleep.
Talons Sharp claws, especially of birds of prey.
Territory An area defended, usually by a male or pair of birds.
Wader A member of the family of shore-birds.
Warbler A member of a group of small song birds.
Wildfowl Ducks, geese and swans.

BEAKS

Short, stout for eating seeds.   Long and thin for catching insects.   Sharp, hooked for tearing flesh.

PARTS OF A BIRD

FEET

Muscular for walking and scratching.   Webbed for swimming.   Sharp talons for clasping prey.

DRAWING A FIELD SKETCH

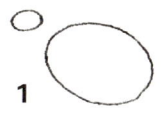 

1. Draw shapes for head and body.
2. Add on other body parts. Draw in any colours, patches or stripes.

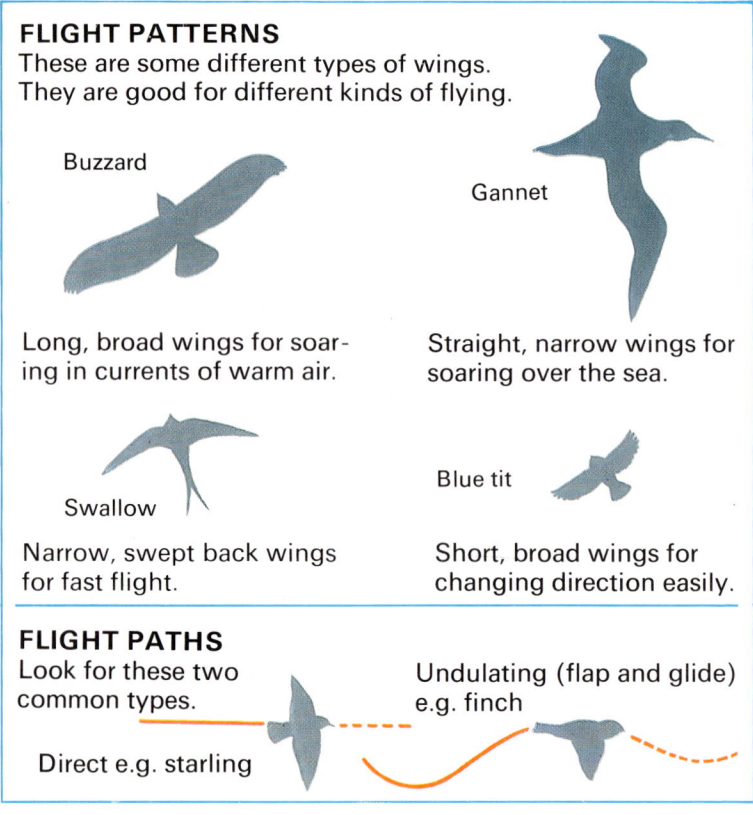

BIRD SONG

Bird song is most obvious in the spring and summer. Male birds sing to attract a mate. A male also sings to signal to other males of his kind to keep out of his territory. They should keep away or run the risk of being attacked.

Singing can also attract predators. This may be why some brightly coloured birds, such as the bullfinch, do not sing very much. Song thrushes sing a lot from tree tops but are hard to spot as they blend in well with the foliage.

Birds living in flocks may have short, simple call notes. This helps to keep the flock together. When alarmed many birds utter sharp calls. These warn all birds around of any possible danger.

DISPLAYS
Displays give messages to both friends and enemies.

Courtship feeding
The female begs for food and that they have formed a pair.

Threat display
The black-headed gull is signalling to its neighbour to keep away.

Distraction display
The lapwing is pretending to be injured. She is trying to take the attention of a predator away from her nest or young.

BATHING AND PREENING

Bathing in water
The blackbird is shuffling its feathers and splashing water onto its back.

Sunbathing
The blackbird is exposing as much of its plumage as possible. Notice that it is panting.

Preening and oiling
After bathing loose feathers have to be preened back into position and smeared with oil from a gland at the base of the tail.

Attracting Birds into the Garden

The illustration should give you plenty of ideas.

1. *Providing food in winter* You may like to make a bird table and provide seeds, peanuts and a variety of kitchen scraps. They can be placed or hung in many ways. Scatter some food under the table for ground-feeding birds. Provide drinking water and replace every hour or so when the ground is frozen.

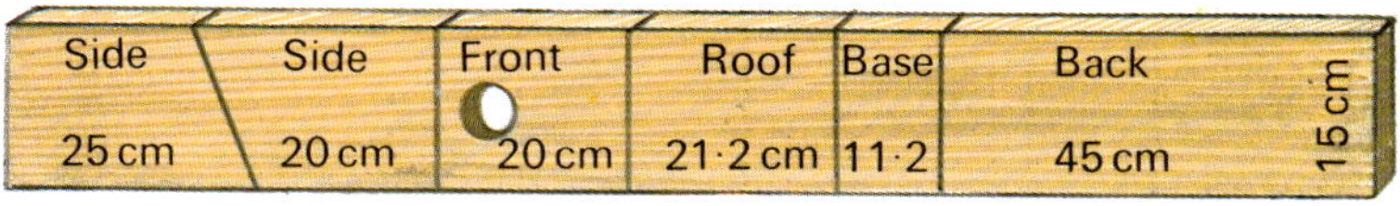

Side	Side	Front	Roof	Base	Back	15 cm
25 cm	20 cm	20 cm	21·2 cm	11·2	45 cm	

2. *Food and cover plants*
Berry-bearing shrubs to grow include hawthorn, elder, ivy and cotoneaster. 'Weeds' such as nettles, dandelions, fathen and brambles are also good foods.

3. *Building a nestbox*
The box can be sited on a tree or wall about 2 metres off the ground. A hole as big as a 10 pence piece will allow blue tits to enter. A slightly larger hole lets great tits in too.

This nestbox is a standard one devised by the RSPB. Ask an adult to help you make it.

How many of these birds can you recognize?

Migration

Summer visitors to Britain usually arrive in April. They stay long enough to breed and raise their young before migrating to warmer climates usually in Africa. Insect-feeding birds, such as swallows, would not find enough food here during our winter.

Birds migrating to Africa usually cross the Mediterranean Sea at its narrowest point. Many of them have to fly across the Sahara desert without feeding. They have to eat well and put on a lot of weight before this journey.

Seabirds leave their colonies in late summer. Puffins go out to sea. Gannets spend the winter in the Bay of Biscay whilst sandwich terns migrate to the west coast of Africa. Adult shelducks go to the Heligoland Bight to moult before returning in early winter.

Winter visitors to Britain arrive from their northern or eastern breeding areas which become covered in ice or snow. Greylag geese journey to Britain from Iceland in flocks of many family parties. The parents, from their past experience, are able to lead their goslings to some of the best feeding and roosting sites in Britain.

Birds do not learn how to migrate. This is shown by young cuckoos which fly to Africa several weeks after the adults have left Britain. Migrants use the Sun and other stars to find their way but how they do so is unknown.

The map opposite shows the general directions travelled by some of the migrants described in this book. Calculate the distances flown and record them in the spaces provided.

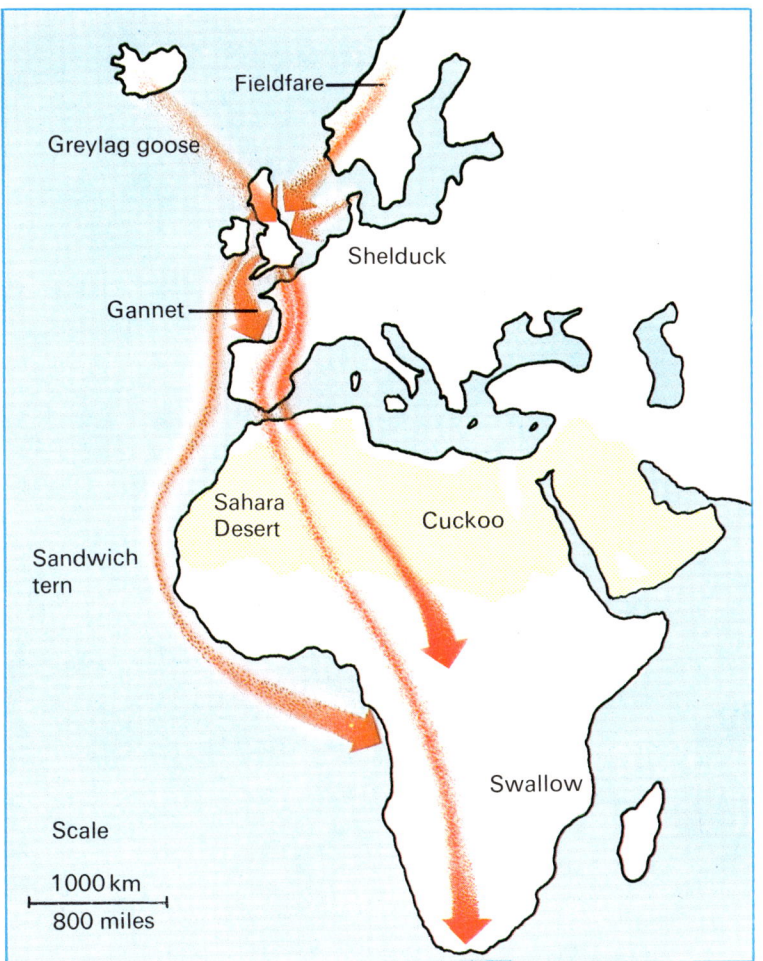

Bird	Distance flown	GANNET	
GREYLAG GOOSE		SANDWICH TERN	
FIELDFARE		SWALLOW	
SHELDUCK		CUCKOO	

Buildings and Gardens

Some birds have adapted well to these habitats, both in town and country. Gardens with trees, shrubs and hedges attract birds such as tits, wrens, and blackbirds. Gardens with plenty of weeds attract seed-loving birds such as sparrows and finches. Sparrows, pigeons and doves often feed on waste foods.

Birds use any song posts they find, including TV aerials, clothes lines, chimneys and fence posts.

Pigeons nest on ledges and house sparrows and starlings under eaves. House martins build their mud nests between walls and eaves. In large cities, kestrels nest high up on office blocks.

You can learn a lot by watching the birds from your window, especially if you provide them with food and nestboxes. Go for walks to see other birds near your home.

BLUE TIT
Look for the blue cap, white face and yellow underparts. Blue tits move quickly and acrobatically amongst the twigs. They peck holes in the tops of milk bottles and drink the cream. When several are together on a bird table, they squabble and display.
Length: 11 cm

DATE _____

PLACE _____

ACTIVITY _____

GREAT TIT

Look for the black head and black stripe through the yellow belly. The stripe is wider in males than females. Note the white cheeks. Great tits search for food low down in trees and on the ground. They also drink from milk bottles.
Length: 13 cm

DATE _____

PLACE _____

ACTIVITY _____

COAL TIT

The head is black with very noticeable white cheek patches and nape. Underparts are buffish-white. Coal tits are fond of taking food from bird tables and hiding it in little stores. They are not as aggressive as other tits.
Length: 11 cm

DATE _____

PLACE _____

ACTIVITY _____

BLACKBIRD
The male is a glossy black with a bright yellow bill. The female is brown. It usually delivers its tuneful song from a high perch at dawn or dusk. When landing, a blackbird cocks up its tail for a few moments. Fond of hopping across lawns in search of earthworms.
Length: 24 cm

DATE _____

PLACE _____

ACTIVITY _____

_____

SONG THRUSH
Brown upperparts and densely spotted underparts. Look for the orange underwing as it flies. It chooses a high perch to sing its repetitive song. Usually seen in ones and twos. Well known for choosing stones and hard paths as 'anvils' where they smash snail shells and eat the contents.
Length: 22 cm

DATE _____

PLACE _____

ACTIVITY _____

_____

ROBIN
Easily recognized by its orange-red breast and face. Upperparts and tail are brown. Becomes very tame in gardens. Robins can be very aggressive towards one another. They display by throwing back their heads and puffing out their breasts into a ball shape.
Length: 13 cm

DATE _____

PLACE _____

ACTIVITY _____

STARLING
Plumage is very dark and speckled. Look for the short tail and pointed wings as it flies. Starlings often flock together, sometimes in thousands. They take over on bird tables. A starling stands upright and walks boldly. Probes in grassy places for grubs. It is noisy, and often mimics other birds.
Length: 21 cm

DATE _____

PLACE _____

ACTIVITY _____

GOLDFINCH

Has a very handsome crimson face mask and brown breast patches. The wide yellow bars on its dark wings show up clearly as it flies. Its flight pattern is undulating (see page 6). It clings to plants such as thistles and quickly extracts the seeds.
Length: 12 cm

DATE _____

PLACE _____

ACTIVITY _____

HOUSE SPARROW

Male has a grey crown and black bib. Both sexes have brown backs with stripes. Calls are usually 'chirps'. Very fond of company. They live near people and commonly nest in the roofs of buildings. They feed mainly on the ground and are fond of grains.
Length: 14 cm

DATE _____

PLACE _____

ACTIVITY _____

DUNNOCK
Look for the slate-coloured head and underparts and the striped brown back. A shy bird usually found at the bottom of hedges or near cover. Has a thin beak and feeds daintily. Fond of feeding under bird tables.
Length: 15 cm

DATE _____

PLACE _____

ACTIVITY _____

GREENFINCH
Male has green underparts and has a brownish/green back. The female is very brown. Both have stout bodies. Look for the yellow wing and tail spots as they fly. In summer, males make continuous 'wheezing' calls. They feed on seeds, found mostly on the ground.
Length: 13 cm

DATE _____

PLACE _____

ACTIVITY _____

HOUSE MARTIN

Upperparts are blue and smoky black and underparts are white. As it flies, look for the white rump and the dark, slightly forked tail. Builds a mud nest, with a small entrance hole, under the eaves of houses. Spends the summer here and the winter in Southern Africa.
Length: 13 cm

DATE _____

PLACE _____

ACTIVITY _____

_____

DOMESTIC PIGEON

These are the domestic forms of the wild rock dove. Some are kept as racing pigeons. Plumage varies greatly – blue, red and white birds are often seen in the same flock. Feral flocks are common in city centres and streets.
Length: 33 cm

DATE _____

PLACE _____

ACTIVITY _____

_____

COLLARED DOVE
Plumage is sandy coloured with a black neck collar. In flight look for the dark wing feathers and white tail band. Flying birds are often closely followed by small birds such as sparrows. Doves are fond of grain. They first came to Britain in 1955 but now are very common.
Length: 27 cm

DATE _____

PLACE _____

ACTIVITY _____

SWALLOW
Look for the red face and throat, and blue back, wings and collar and deeply forked tail. It builds an open nest of mud, often inside buildings. Flies fast and low to catch insects. In autumn, before migrating to Southern Africa, large flocks gather on telegraph wires.
Length: 19 cm

DATE _____

PLACE _____

ACTIVITY _____

Woodlands

The best woods for birds are those which contain many kinds of plants. These usually grow in four layers – large trees; shrubs and bushes; brambles, ferns and nettles; and a ground layer of mosses and grass. You will see all these layers in a mixed oak wood.

Forests planted with fir trees have many kinds of plants in them when the trees are small. As the fir trees grow up and the other plants die off, many birds move away.

You have to be very patient when bird-watching in woods. A good plan is to sit quietly and wait for the birds to show themselves. Choose areas that overlook clearings, fire breaks, streams or damp spots. Woods always seem full of bird noises. Try to match the songs with their owners.

TAWNY OWL
Britain's commonest owl, although it is not found in Ireland. It is also called brown or wood owl. Has a large rounded head with both black eyes pointing forward. Look for the feathery feet. It is a night bird, but during the day it may be set on by groups of small birds. Often heard hooting in the evening. It feeds on insects, smaller birds and mice.
Length: 38 cm

DATE _____

PLACE _____

ACTIVITY _____

GREEN WOODPECKER

Upper body green and underparts yellow. The red crown and black face are very striking. Look for the yellow rump as it flies. It is often seen on the ground in clearings and grassy areas where it feeds on ants. Its call is a loud laughing cry.
Length: 30 cm

DATE _____

PLACE _____

ACTIVITY _____

_____

SPARROWHAWK

Male has a light brown barred underside and bluish back. Female is larger and has a brown back. Both have barred tails and underwings. Look for the short rounded wings. Flies with rapid wing-beats and catches small birds along hedges and the edges of woods.
Length: 30–40 cm

DATE _____

PLACE _____

ACTIVITY _____

_____

CHAFFINCH

The male has a chestnut breast and a blue-grey head. The female is greenish-brown. Look for the large white wing patches and white outer tail feathers as they fly. Call is usually 'pink ... pink'. They are often seen feeding on the ground, sometimes in large flocks in the winter.
Length: 15 cm

DATE _____

PLACE _____

ACTIVITY _____

_____

BULLFINCH

The male has red underparts, and the female has grey-brown underparts. Both sexes have black caps and stout bills. Look for the dark wings with white stripes and the white rump as it flies. In winter they may form small flocks. They feed on fruits, seeds and buds.
Length: 14 cm

DATE _____

PLACE _____

ACTIVITY _____

_____

CHIFFCHAFF
A very common warbler which breeds in Britain but migrates to Africa for the winter. The greenish-brown plumage helps it blend with leaves and twigs. It is more often heard than seen. Its call is a repeated 'chiff chaff'. It feeds on small insects.
Length: 10 cm

DATE _____

PLACE _____

ACTIVITY _____

WREN
A small, restless brown bird instantly recognized by its short, upright tail. It has a surprisingly loud song which can be heard a long way off. It feeds on small insects caught in the undergrowth. In winter several birds have been known to roost in the same nestbox.
Length: 10 cm

DATE _____

PLACE _____

ACTIVITY _____

Open Spaces

Most open spaces – fields and playing fields – have been made by people, yet many birds thrive on them. Kestrels hunt for voles and mice, even along the grassy edges of motorways. Black-headed gulls roost on playing fields, especially when puddles form after wet weather.

The four members of the crow family (pages 26–27) live on farmland especially if it contains large hedges and small woods. Wood pigeons, pheasants, crows, and flocks of sparrows and finches like fields of crops. They eat waste grains and weed seeds. Ploughed fields often attract large flocks of birds, particularly black-headed gulls.

KESTREL
The male has a blue head, reddish back and wings with dark spots. It has a black band at base of its blue tail. The female is mostly brown. Often hovers, with tail fanned, about 10 metres above the ground whilst searching for prey. Look for the pointed wings, long tail, hooked beak and sharp talons.
Length: 30–32 cm

DATE _____

PLACE _____

ACTIVITY _____

_____

WOOD PIGEON

Blue body with pink breast and black tail tip. Look for the white neck mark and wing bar as it flies. Eats grain and grazes clover. At dusk, flocks of many thousands fly into woods to roost. Very shy in the country but much tamer in towns.
Length: 40 cm

DATE _____

PLACE _____

ACTIVITY _____

PHEASANT

The male has gaudy body plumage. The female is light brown and smaller. Look for their very long tails and strong legs. They feed on seeds, especially grains. One male may be seen with several females. They flap violently when taking off and then glide for some distance.
Length: 82 cm

DATE _____

PLACE _____

ACTIVITY _____

ROOK
Has a glossy black plumage with a fairly long straight beak. The pale base of the beak helps to tell it apart from other crows. Look for the very loosely feathered thighs as it walks. Nests in large groups called rookeries. Found in flocks throughout the year. Its 'caw' is less harsh than a crow's.
Length: 44 cm

DATE _____

PLACE _____

ACTIVITY _____

_____

CARRION CROW
All black with only a little gloss. Its beak is quite heavy and slightly curved. Usually seen in ones and twos. It nests in trees or on cliffs. In Scotland and Ireland the plumage is grey and black, and it is known there as the hooded crow. Makes a harsh 'caw' sound.
Length: 44 cm

DATE _____

PLACE _____

ACTIVITY _____

_____

MAGPIE

The black and white plumage and long tail are easy to spot. Flies with fast flaps followed by short glides. Usually seen in ones or twos but larger numbers roost together. Its call is a fast, harsh chatter. Its nest is large and domed with a small side entrance.
Length: 44 cm

DATE _____

PLACE _____

ACTIVITY _____

JACKDAW

A small crow with grey on the nape, sides of the face and on the underparts. Flies with fast wing beats, often acrobatically and in small flocks. Struts around on land with head bobbing. Makes nest in holes in trees, buildings, and sometimes down chimney pots. Its call usually sounds as 'jack jack'.
Length: 32 cm

DATE _____

PLACE _____

ACTIVITY _____

LAPWING

Upperparts are dark and the underparts dark and white. Its curved head-crest is easy to spot. The broad and rounded wings can be clearly seen as it flies. Its flight is clumsy and uneven. Large flocks build up in winter. It is sometimes called a 'pee-wit' after its call. It is fond of eating insect larvae.
Length: 30 cm

DATE _____

PLACE _____

ACTIVITY _____

_____

PIED WAGTAIL

Small black and white bird with a long, constantly wagging tail and bobbing head. Runs very quickly to catch insects. Mostly seen in small groups, but large numbers gather together to roost. They sometimes attack their own reflections in car hubcaps.
Length: 18 cm

DATE _____

PLACE _____

ACTIVITY _____

_____

FIELDFARE
This thrush has a very grey head and rump, reddish-brown back and spotted breast. Look for its very dark tail and sides of the face. They breed in Scandinavia and Eastern Europe and spend the autumn and winter in Britain.
Length: 24 cm

DATE _____

PLACE _____

ACTIVITY _____

BLACK-HEADED GULL
A small gull with a white body, a grey back and grey upper wings. In summer, it has a brownish head, but in winter it has no more than a dark spot on its head. If it is standing, look for its red beak and legs. Flocks often follow the plough and feed on worms and larvae. Breeds in crowded, noisy colonies.
Length: 34 cm

DATE _____

PLACE _____

ACTIVITY _____

Moors and Heaths

Moors and heaths are very open areas, with large expanses of ling or heather and coarse grass. Most moorland is in the north and west of Britain where there is a lot of rain. Large areas are often burned to make room for young heather shoots – the favourite food of red grouse.

Heaths are found in the drier lowland areas of Britain. Bracken and gorse are sometimes common.

You will not usually see very many birds on moors and heaths. When walking along keep your eyes on the horizon to catch glimpses of any large birds. Birds hidden in nearby heather may also fly up. When travelling by car, stop from time to time, especially alongside marshy areas. Use binoculars to scan for distant birds.

STONECHAT
The male has an obvious black hood and orange-brown underparts and white neck mark. The female is less brightly coloured and does not have the white rump of the male. Perches in an upright manner and often sings from the tops of bushes and small trees.
Length: 12 cm

DATE _____

PLACE _____

ACTIVITY _____

SKYLARK

The body is well covered with brown stripy spots. It has a small head crest and a fairly long tail. Often seen singing, high above the ground, appearing to hang in the same spot for some time. Look for the white outer tail feathers as it flies. Eats seeds and insects on the ground.
Length: 18 cm

DATE _____

PLACE _____

ACTIVITY _____

_____

CUCKOO

The male's upperparts are grey and the female's are brown. Both have barred underparts. Look for the long wings and tail. The 'cuckoo' call is made by the male; the female babbles. She lays her eggs in the nests of other birds who then rear the young cuckoos. Spends the winter in Africa.
Length: 32 cm

DATE _____

PLACE _____

ACTIVITY _____

_____

MERLIN
A small falcon. The male has a blue back and tail. The female is slightly larger and has a brown back and tail. They fly fast and low over the ground. Often seen perching on large stones or posts. They feed on small birds.
Length: 28–30 cm

DATE _____

PLACE _____

ACTIVITY _____

_____

BUZZARD
Upperparts usually brown and underparts streaked with brown. If it is flying look for the broad rounded wings with dark patches; small head and rounded tail. Fond of soaring. Usually silent but has a piercing 'mew' call. Feeds on small animals and carrion.
Length: 48–53 cm

DATE _____

PLACE _____

ACTIVITY _____

_____

RED GROUSE

A plump-bodied game bird with reddish-brown plumage. Females are usually paler than males. Look for the red patch over the eye. In flight the wings and tail seem dark. Flies rapidly with a whirring noise and then glides. Mostly feeds on heather shoots. Will not be seen in most of Southern England.
Length: 32–37 cm

DATE _____

PLACE _____

ACTIVITY _____

Freshwaters

Reservoirs, pits, ponds and lakes are excellent places to watch birds. During the day, grebes dive out in the open water for small fish and water beetles. Coots dive for water plants which they carefully pick through on the surface. Mallards up-end for seeds under the surface. Swans often walk onto the banks to graze on soft grasses. In the evening, geese and gulls may fly in to roost.

Waterbirds make a variety of grunts and quacks. Try and match up any noises you hear with the birds you see. Look at any patches of reeds. In summer, coots and moorhens may be feeding their young. In late summer, reed beds are important roosts for swallows, and in winter for large flocks of starlings.

HERON

Very large grey bird with long legs, long neck and dagger-like beak. When flying, it beats its wings very slowly. It stands very still then suddenly darts out its head to catch fish and frogs.
Length: 90 cm

DATE _____

PLACE _____

ACTIVITY _____

GREYLAG GOOSE
The largest 'grey' goose. Look for the pink legs and orange beak. The forewing as it flies is light grey. Note the V shape of a flock in flight. Wild geese breed in Iceland and migrate to Britain for the winter. There are many feral flocks in lowland areas. Feeds and roosts in flocks. This goose is the ancestor of the farmyard goose.
Length: 80 cm

DATE _____

PLACE _____

ACTIVITY _____

MOORHEN
It has a black body with a red beak and face. Look for the white stripe on the flank and under its tail. If often jerks its tail and bobs its head when swimming or walking. On land, look for its very long toes which make it look awkward. Moorhens often threaten one another.
Length: 32 cm

DATE _____

PLACE _____

ACTIVITY _____

MUTE SWAN

This is the largest British bird. It is all white, but note the black knob at the base of its orange-red beak, larger in the male than the female. Parents hiss and arch their wings when protecting the grey-coloured cygnets. Runs along the water before taking off. Skis to a halt on landing.
Length: 140 cm

DATE _____

PLACE _____

ACTIVITY _____

_____

GREAT-CRESTED GREBE

Very pointed head with a long pinkish beak. It has a long, straight white neck. Its plumage is basically brown and white. Note its eartufts in summer. Its feet trail behind its body as it flies. It makes elaborate displays when courting. Chicks sometimes ride around on their parents' backs.
Length: 45 cm

DATE _____

PLACE _____

ACTIVITY _____

_____

COOT

This bird is all black with a white beak and white on the front of its head. It takes off after a long run along the water. As it flies, its feet dangle under it. It has flaps along each toe. It walks fairly easily and may leave the water to graze on the banks. Coots gather into large flocks in winter.
Length: 36 cm

DATE _____

PLACE _____

ACTIVITY _____

MALLARD

The male has a green head, yellowish beak and chestnut brown breast. The female is all brown. Both have a blue wing patch. Mallards walk easily on land . Look for the orange legs and webbed feet. The female rears ducklings alone. Mallards are the wild ancestors of our domestic ducks.
Length: 58 cm

DATE _____

PLACE _____

ACTIVITY _____

Coastal Areas

Britain is famous for its large colonies of breeding seabirds, especially on the steeper cliffs in the north and west. Watching their activities from a safe spot is very exciting. There is much coming and going at the noisy breeding ledges. Boat trips around seabird islands are worth going on.

Try to identify as many gulls as you can. Look along tide-lines, on piers and closely behind any fishing boats bringing in their catch.

In winter and spring our estuaries hold thousands of waders, such as curlews, and wildfowl, such as shelduck. You can watch safely from old sea-walls and banks. When the tide is in waders roost in large flocks. As the tide goes out they follow, fanning out to feed in the damp sand and wet mud.

PUFFIN
It has a plump body with white underparts and a black back and wings. It has a white face and its large beak is brightly coloured in the summer. Flies low over water with quick beats of its short wings. Swims under water and catches small fish. Breeds in colonies.
Length: 30 cm

DATE _____

PLACE _____

ACTIVITY _____

HERRING GULL

Adults are white underneath, with grey backs and upper wings. Wing tips are black. Young birds are very brown. When it is standing, look for the yellow beak and pink legs. Fond of soaring high overhead. Feeds along tide lines and follows fishing boats.
Length: 56 cm

DATE _____

PLACE _____

ACTIVITY _____

_____

GANNET

These large white birds have dark wing tips. Younger birds are brown. Beats its wings stiffly. Dives into the sea with bent wings from about 20 metres and catches fish in its dagger-like beak. Sometimes follows fishing boats.
Length: 90 cm

DATE _____

PLACE _____

ACTIVITY _____

_____

CORMORANT
This large blackish bird is fond of standing on rocks or posts. It holds its wings half open to dry out its feathers. Look for the long, slightly hooked beak and white chin. Breeding birds have a white thigh patch. Cormorants fly low over the water. They swim and dive for fish.
Length: 90 cm

DATE _____

PLACE _____

ACTIVITY _____

_____

SHELDUCK
A very handsome duck with dark green, black, chestnut and white plumage. The male has a red knob at the base of the beak. Searches for small snails in damp mud. Fond of nesting in old rabbit burrows.
Length: 60 cm

DATE _____

PLACE _____

ACTIVITY _____

_____

OYSTERCATCHER

The glossy black and white plumage, long orange beak and reddish legs are easy to spot. Look for the broad white wing bar as it flies. Breeds along most coasts. Large flocks can be seen in estuaries in winter. Feeds on worms and shellfish.
Length: 42 cm

DATE _____

PLACE _____

ACTIVITY _____

CURLEW

Look for the long legs and very long down-curved beak. Its plumage is mainly brown stripy spots. Large flocks spend the winter in estuaries. They probe into soft mud for worms. Named after its call – a mellow 'curlee'.
Length: 54 cm

DATE _____

PLACE _____

ACTIVITY _____

Nature Reserves

Many of the best examples of the habitats considered in this book are now kept as nature reserves; some specially for birds. Some hold large colonies of breeding seabirds such as gannets and sandwich terns. Others hold large numbers of wintering waterfowl, such as wild geese and swans. Rare breeding birds such as ospreys or red kites need reserved areas where they are protected from egg collectors and vandals.

Almost all the bitterns in Britain are found at reed-bed nature reserves, which are kept as wet as possible in the summer. Avocets, ruff and black-tailed godwits, which have all recently returned to Britain, are conserved on wet grasslands and marshes.

Most nature reserves have hides so that people can see the birds close to. Many also have nature trails.

RED KITE
Its plumage is red-brown. Look for the forked tail and white patches on its wings as it flies. They were common in Britain until about 1800, but they are now found only in a small area in Wales. They breed on wooded hillsides, and are fond of feeding on carrion.
Length: 60 cm

DATE _____

PLACE _____

ACTIVITY _____
_____

OSPREY

Upperparts are dark with a white crown. Underparts mostly white with close barring on wings and tail. In flight, wings are slightly arched and bent. Plunges feet first into water to catch fish. Look for its very powerful talons. It has bred in Scotland over the last 25 years. It spends the winter in Africa.
Length: 60 cm

DATE _____

PLACE _____

ACTIVITY _____

BITTERN

Streaky brown plumage with black cap. A very shy bird but may sometimes be seen flying low over reed beds, mainly in Eastern England. In spring, the male makes a 'booming' noise which can be heard up to 5 kilometres away.
Length: 75 cm

DATE _____

PLACE _____

ACTIVITY _____

SANDWICH TERN

Plumage is grey and white. Look for the black legs, beak, head and crest. Its beak is tipped with yellow. They breed in dense, noisy colonies. Plunge dive into the sea for small fish. They spend the winter off the West Coast of Africa.
Length: 40 cm

DATE _____

PLACE _____

ACTIVITY _____

_____

BLACK-TAILED GODWIT

In summer the head, neck and breast are chestnut. At other times the plumage is grey-brown. Notice the long straight beak and legs. Look for the white wing bars and rump and black tail band as it flies. Breeds at a few wet meadow sites.
Length: 40 cm

DATE _____

PLACE _____

ACTIVITY _____

_____

AVOCET

A very elegant black and white shore-bird with very long blue legs and a long black upturned beak. It flies gracefully with slow wing beats. It breeds at a few coastal marshes in Eastern England where it is protected. Feeds on small water animals.
Length: 45 cm

DATE _____

PLACE _____

ACTIVITY _____

_____

RUFF

In summer only the males have well developed ruffs or collars of different colours. The females are much smaller. Both sexes have scaly, brown patterns on their backs. They breed at a few wetlands in Britain and spend the winter in Africa. At breeding time the males gather together to display.
Length: 22–30 cm

DATE _____

PLACE _____

ACTIVITY _____

_____

Bird Conservation

The countryside is changing and some of the habitats considered in this book face uncertain futures. Heaths and woodlands are disappearing fast. They are being turned into farmland or are being built on. Most of our natural wetlands have been drained and turned into farmland. Some birds can live only in these habitats and are unable to survive these changes.

Some of our common birds, however, have adapted quite well to change. Many which originally lived only in woodland are able to breed and feed around houses and gardens. Some waterbirds are able to live on some of the many reservoirs and gravel pits that we have created.

We are fortunate in still having some large moors, open spaces, estuaries and unspoilt cliffs. Bird conservationists try to ensure that the most important habitats are not destroyed. Sometimes they buy them and run them as nature reserves.

Each year, oil pollution in the sea kills thousands of seabirds such as puffins. This is sometimes caused by a shipwrecked oil tanker, but all types of ships release their used engine oil into the sea.

Some agricultural pesticides can be very damaging to birds. Ten to twenty years ago DDT and similar chemicals were widely used in Britain. They killed many thousands of small birds. They also killed the kestrels and sparrow hawks which ate the poisoned birds.

Some birds are very easily disturbed. Nesting birds desert their eggs and young if people spend too much time near them. In winter, when food may be scarce many birds feed during all the daylight hours. They would starve if disturbed. If you realize that you are disturbing a bird, you should move away as quickly as you can.

Where to Go From Here

Having looked at your local birds and at birds further afield, you will realize that many birds have not been mentioned in this book. If you take up bird-watching seriously, you will need a field guide that includes every bird. You will also need binoculars.

You can meet up with other local bird-watchers by contacting your local bird club or natural history society. Their addresses will be in your local library. National organizations are listed below. If you write for any details, please enclose a stamped addressed envelope.

Royal Society for the Protection of Birds (RSPB), The Lodge, Sandy, Beds SG19 2DL. Owns or leases over 80 nature reserves. Carries out education and conservation work. Members receive the quarterly magazine *Birds* and free entry to reserves.

Young Ornithologists' Club (YOC), The Lodge, Sandy, Beds SG19 2DL. Organization run by the RSPB for young people up to 18 years old. YOC leaders nationwide organize indoor and outdoor meetings. Members receive bi-monthly magazine *Bird Life*, arm badge and card. Projects and competitions organized. Individual and group membership available.

Wildfowl and Wetlands Trust, Slimbridge, Glos GL2 7BT. Runs eight centres showing wildfowl collections or wild refuges. Carries out research and conservation work. Members receive the *Wildfowl and Wetlands Magazine* twice a year and free entry to Trust centres. Family membership available.

British Trust for Ornithology (BTO), Beech Grove, Tring, Herts HP23 5NR. Organizes research into the status and distribution of birds. Members receive *BTO News*. Junior membership available.

Index

Avocet 42, 45

Bathing 7
Beaks 5
Bird table 8
Bird song 6
Bittern 42, 43
Blackbird 7, 12, 14
Black-headed gull 7, 24, 29
Black-tailed godwit 42, 44
Blue tit 6, 12
Bullfinch 6, 22
Buzzard 6, 32/33

Carrion crow 26
Chaffinch 5, 22
Chiffchaff 23
Coal tit 13
Collared dove 19
Coot 34, 37
Cormorant 40
Cuckoo 10, 11, 31
Curlew 38, 41

Displays 7
Domestic pigeon 12, 18
Dunnock 17

Feet 5
Fieldfare 11, 29
Field sketch 4, 5
Flight: paths 6; patterns 6

Gannet 6, 10, 11, 39
Goldfinch 16
Great-crested grebe 36
Great tit 13
Greenfinch 17
Green woodpecker 21
Greylag goose 10, 11, 35

Habitats 4, 12, 20, 24, 30, 34, 38, 42, 46
Heron 34

Herring gull 39
House martin 12, 18
House sparrow 12, 16

Jackdaw 27

Kestrel 1, 12, 24, 46

Lapwing 7, 28

Magpie 2, 27
Mallard 34, 37
Merlin 32
Moorhen 34, 35
Mute swan 36

Nestbox 9

Osprey 42, 43
Oystercatcher 41

Pheasant 24, 25
Pied wagtail 28
Preening 7
Puffin 10, 38, 46

Red grouse 33
Red kite 42
Robin 15
Rook 26
Ruff 42, 45

Sandwich tern 10, 11, 44
Shelduck 10, 11, 38, 40
Skylark 31
Song thrush 6, 14
Sparrowhawk 21, 46
Starling 6, 7, 12, 15, 34
Stonechat 30
Swallow 6, 10, 11, 19, 34

Tawny owl 20

Wings 6
Wood pigeon 24, 25
Wren 12, 23